Sonoran Desert Food Plants
Edible Uses for the Desert's Wil

MW00773587

Lincoln Town Press
All rights reserved
Copyright © 2011, 2017 by Charles W. Kane
Second edition: September 2017
Library of Congress Control Number: 2017909723
ISBN 10: 0998287121 and ISBN 13: 9780998287126

Printed and bound in the United States of America

Additional titles by Charles W. Kane
Medicinal Plants of the Western Mountain States (9780998287102)
Medicinal Plants of the American Southwest (9780977133376)
Herbal Medicine: Trends and Traditions (9780977133321)
Southern California Food Plants (9780977133383)
Wild Edible Plants of Texas (9780977133390)

Introduction

Scope

Sonoran Desert Food Plants is specifically designed as an introduction to the wild edible plant life of the Sonoran Desert. Although I have included as much information as possible (only so much can be covered in 64 pages), for the serious student, consider this booklet a primer. For the newly interested, it is a suggestion that the wild plant world is not only a nice thing to behold, but something to interact with that has real utilitarian value.

Certainly, some of these plants have medicinal uses; however, I've kept this element to a minimum – not everyone who has interest in wild food shares the same for medicine. And generally speaking, if a plant is edible it will have low to no medicinal use. After all, a plant's chemistry defines it's potential: complexity and strength denotes medicine. Ubiquity and mildness suggests food. The two realms are often mutually exclusive.

The Sonoran Desert

This arid desert region (approximately 3000' and below) ranges from central/southern Arizona, west to adjacent California state line regions, and south into Baja California and Sonora Mexico. The following profiles cover plants found within the United States (there are many edible Sonoran Desert plants that grow only south of the border – these are not necessarily covered). Additionally, a number of plants covered herein have wider ranges; many are found throughout the Greater Southwest and even country–wide.

First Tier Plant Versus Second Tier Plant

Almost any plant/plant–part can be dried, boiled, cooked, roasted, or denatured in some way in order to be made more or less 'edible' for true survival situations. Even lawn clippings, old leather, and nutrient rich soils can be ingested (or mouthed) with the intent of warding off starvation for another day or two. These items and items like them represent 'second tier plants' (or otherwise). They are not the focus of this work.

The majority of subjects profiled are plants that provide nutrients AND calories, in the form of protein, carbohydrates, and fats, and only then vitamins, minerals, micronutrients, etc. (and not the reverse). This distinction, between first tier plant (supplying calories and important nutrients) vs. second tier plant (supping chlorophyll, fiber, and some nutritional components, yet low to no calories) is often omitted by many edible plant authorities, as if the race to list as many plants (or plant parts) as possible precludes a coherent hierarchy – again, lawn clippings are 'edible', but should they be chucked in with better wild foods just for the sake of a long plant list?

In the ever–changing world in which we live, there may come an unfortunate period, triggered by unforeseen events, when days are measured by the symptoms of starvation and lack. This will be precisely the time not to have questions about edible plant relevancy. Be smart about it – know the important sustenance providers...first.

Proper Identification

Do not eat any plant if uncertain of its identity! Although fatal mistakes are rare (usually someone will only be temporarily sickened), they are possible with the ingestion of a handful of plants found throughout the Sonoran region.

Know your poisonous Carrot family plants (namely Poison hemlock, which is not common to the area, but may still be encountered around water and damp areas) and toxic nightshades (Tobacco and Datura). A number of Pea family plants (Coral bean and Loco weed for instance) and members of the Borage family (Fiddleneck and Popcorn flower) are also known harborers of poisonous compounds.

Along with this booklet, the use of several field guides (or the instruction of an expert) to confirm identification is optimal in most cases. The take–away: THERE SHOULD BE NO DOUBT OF A PLANT'S IDENTITY BEFORE CONSUMPTION.

Acknowledgments

While many contributions and assists have helped propel this material, no acknowledgment would be complete without giving thanks to Superstition Mountain man Peter Bigfoot. His depth and understanding of the edible plant field stands unequaled.

Wendy C. Hodgson's Food Plants of the Sonoran Desert, Richard Felger's and Mary Moser's People of the Desert and Sea, and At the Desert's Green Edge by Amadeo M. Rea are just several texts that were used in rounding out the material in this booklet. I also recommend these books for a deeper ethnobotanical/historical appreciation of the following Sonoran Desert food plants.

A Few Plants to Avoid

(the following are a small number of poisonous plants; they are best avoided)

Poison hemlock (Conium)

Poison hemlock (Conium)

Coral bean (Erythrina)

Datura

Tree tobacco (Nicotiana)

Desert tobacco (Nicotiana)

Agave
Agave spp.

Other Common Names
Century plant, Maguey

Range & Habitat
Common throughout the Sonoran Uplands, look for Agave on rocky slopes and hillsides. Agave parryi, A. palmeri, and A. chrysantha are the wider–ranging species of Arizona.

Edible Uses
Just as the developing flower stalk begins to emerge the plant is uprooted and the leaves cut from the core as close to the base as possible – the 'heart' or core (along with the lower immature stalk and leaf bases) is the main food part. If in the field, a baking pit needs to be constructed where the core/lower stalk/leaf bases are baked for at least 24 hours. If lacking a baking pit, these parts (wrapped in foil) can also be baked (300–350 degrees) in a conventional oven for the better part of a day. If collected in season and cooked thoroughly, the result will be a more–or–less sweetish, semi–fibrous mass that can be sliced and eaten. The cooking process for Agave is important – heat converts the plant's complex starches (bitter–soapy) into simple sugars (sweet). Other Agave species serve as base materials for Tequila, Pulque (a fermented/alcoholic beverage), and syrup.

Cautions & Special Note
The fresh leaf sap is often found irritating to the skin. Indigestion issues can arise if the core has not been sufficiently cooked, the plant was collected out–of–season, or large amounts are eaten at one time.

For Agave cordage: clip the leaves from the base when green. Air dry, then pound/twist the leaves to separate the fibers from the surrounding leaf material. The dried out–of–season core and stem base were once utilized as a primitive soap (due to saponins).

Sustenance Index: High
Pictured: *Agave chrysantha* (top) | *Agave lecheguilla* (bottom)

Amaranth
Amaranthus spp.

Other Common Names
Pigweed, Carelessweed, Quelites

Range & Habitat
Amaranth is common throughout the Southwest. In the Sonoran Desert look to lower–lying moist soils, such as old fields, ditches, and roadsides. Amaranthus palmeri is the most abundantly encountered species. It grows quickly in response to monsoon rains.

Edible Uses
As one of our more palatable greens, most species of Amaranth are utilizable. The summertime young leaves are eaten raw directly from the plant or used as a salad ingredient; however, they can be eaten in larger quantities if first steamed, lightly sautéed, or boiled. The leaves taste much like spinach once cooked.

After Amaranth has gone to seed (late summer–fall), strip the dried seed spikes from the top of each plant. Wearing gloves, rub the clusters together to separate the seeds from their spiky encasements. Winnow in a light breeze. The seeds are high in protein and generally nutritious. They can be ground into a meal, cooked like other grains, or soaked and then eaten.

Medicinal Uses
Amaranth has no significant medicinal use.

Cautions
There are no cautions for Amaranth.

Special Note
Cultivated species were once important Mesoamerican food (seed) crops. Love–lies–bleeding (Amaranthus caudatus) is one the more popular ornamental Amaranths.

Sustenance Index: High

Pictured: *Amaranthus hybridus* (top) | *Amaranthus palmeri* (bottom)

Arizona Jewel Flower
Streptanthus carinatus

Other Common Names
Twistflower, Jewelflower

Range & Habitat
An early spring desert annual, Arizona jewel flower is most commonly encountered from Pima County, then east through New Mexico, to Texas.

Edible Uses
Belonging to the Mustard family, the entire above–ground portion is edible, particularly when young. Spicy and pungent, limited amounts can be eaten raw: as a garnish, salad accent, or trail–nibble.

Like any Mustard green, Arizona jewel flower is best steamed, sautéed, or boiled. Once heat is used to dissipate the plant's potentially irritating volatiles, larger amounts are consumed problem–free.

Further along in the season (late spring) the seeds are gathered as a Mustard seed substitute. They should be dried and powered and used as a spice, as the whole seeds, chewed and eaten, are extremely spicy and may cause mouth/throat burning.

Medicinal Uses
Eat a small handful of the fresh leaf if suffering from indigestion (not heartburn). Most Mustards are mildly diuretic and have been long–used in kidney stone disturbances.

Cautions & Special Note
Eating large quantities of Arizona jewel flower (especially fresh) may cause kidney sensitivity and in some women stimulant menses. Both the medicinal uses and cautions for this plant are dependent upon volatile compounds called glucosinolates, a.k.a. 'Mustard oil'.

Sustenance Index: Low
Pictured: *Streptanthus carinatus*

Asian Mustard
Brassica tournefortii

Other Common Names
African mustard, Moroccan mustard

Range & Habitat
Asian mustard is originally from the Old World – Europe, Asia, and Africa. First recorded in California in 1941, and then Arizona in 1959, its presence across the Southwest has since greatly expanded. Arizona and Nevada list it as an invasive weed. Low elevation areas where the soil has once been disturbed are its typical places: roadsides, old fields, ditches, etc.

Edible Uses
Of the four Mustard family plants profiled in this booklet, Asian mustard is likely the least palatable. I recommend skipping the plant's mature leaves, which are coarse, semi–fibrous, and mildly bitter, and instead gather only the very young leaves and/or young flowering stem tops. These parts will have a mustard flavor but less of the mentioned poor qualities.

Use Asian mustard fresh in small amounts as a salad accent or garnish. First steamed, sautéed, or boiled, it's fine eaten in larger amounts.

Like Arizona jewel flower and London Rocket, Asian mustard's seeds can be used as a Mustard seed substitute. Being very small though, having access to a sizable patch is necessary. Once the slim and linear seed pod is formed and just beginning to tan (mid–spring), snip the entire stem top from the plant. Place the tops in a paper bag. Once dry, hand garble the seed pods, separating the pod from the seed. Winnow in a light breeze. Repeat.

Medicinal Uses & Cautions
See Arizona jewel flower for Asian mustard's medicinal uses/cautions. They are the same.

Barrel Cactus

Ferocactus wislizeni

Other Common Names
Fishhook barrel cactus, Compass cactus, Candy barrel cactus

Range & Habitat
Barrel cactus is found throughout desert elevations of Arizona and southwestern New Mexico.

Edible Uses
Barrel cactus fruit take a number of months to ripen fully (yellow) and can remain on the cactus for up to a year (usually about 6 months). The outer flesh is mildly tart and a bit mucilaginous. It is eaten either raw or cooked. The black seeds of the mature fruit are eaten as is, or dried and ground into a meal. Compared to the flesh, they contain greater protein quantities and therefore should be considered the more nutritious part of the fruit. Due to the absence of small thorns or glochids, Barrel cactus is easier to gather/eat than other cacti.

Medicinal Uses
There are no significant medicinal uses for Barrel cactus.

Cautions
There are no cautions for Barrel cactus fruit.

Special Note
Apart from extreme emergency, sourcing 'water' via straining Barrel cactus' internal pulp is not recommended. To the non–acclimated, drinking this cactus juice may cause digestive upset, diarrhea, and possible vomiting, speeding up the body's dehydration if in a survival situation. Gathering the internal pulp also kills the cactus.

Barrel cactus *very generally* leans southward to southwestward. Before striking out in any direction, get a consensus from a group of Barrel cactus if lost without a compass.

Sustenance Index: High
Pictured: *Ferocactus wislizeni*

Beargrass
Nolina microcarpa

Other Common Names
Sacahuista

Range & Habitat
Beargrass comprises just one Nolina species found throughout the Greater Southwest. It ranges from southwestern Utah through to most of the Desert Grassland elevations of Arizona and New Mexico. Several species are also found in the Southeast.

Edible Uses
The immature flower stalk is a fair edible. Early in the season, clip the stalk at its base when 1'–2' tall and still flexible. Peel the outer skin from the stalk and eat the center material as is, or if bitter, chop, boil, and rinse it with fresh water. The stalk can also be wrapped in foil and roasted over coals. As the stalk ages, it becomes more woody, bitter, and soapy. Desert spoon (Dasylirion wheeleri) can be collected and prepared the same way as Beargrass.

Medicinal Uses
Beargrass roots have potential anti-inflammatory/anti–arthritic effects like Yucca. Additionally, due to its array of medicinal saponins, applied externally, it's a fair remedy for varicose veins.

Cautions
If the stalks are overly bitter and soapy, digestive upset is possible if consumed in large amounts.

Special Note
Beargrass' leaves maintain their flexibility after drying, making them a choice article in basket weaving, broom making, and other similar applications. A wash made with the roots, like Yucca, will lather to some degree, making a weak soap solution.

Sustenance Index: Medium
Pictured: *Nolina microcarpa*

Biscuitroot

Lomatium nevadense

Other Common Names
Spring parsley, Desert parsley, Nevada biscuitroot

Range & Habitat
Biscuitroot is common throughout much of Arizona. It's almost always found in upper desert zones on rocky hillsides and slopes. New Mexico, Utah, California, Nevada, Idaho, and Oregon also host the plant.

Edible Uses
The young herbage can be eaten raw, or better yet, boiled or steamed and consumed as a cooked green.

The roots of Biscuitroot are usually thickened and non–woody. Depending on soil conditions, they take on a variety of forms, but one of the more common shapes is as a bulbous–storage mass (at the root's end). Ideally the roots are starchy and taste like a bland parsnip. They can sometimes too be a little acrid, astringent, and fibrous – boiling/cooking will render them more palatable. They are a good complex carbohydrate source.

Medicinal Uses & Cautions
This species of Biscuitroot is not medicinal; however, L. dissectum (non–edible) represents the most common medicinal species within the genus (see Medicinal Plants of the Western Mountain States for a complete discussion). Lomatium dissectum (and any other Lomatium species with resinous, balsamic, and bitter tasting roots) is an important lung medicine. In general, the medicinal species of Lomatium tend to be larger plants with deeper–reaching and bigger roots.

Sustenance Index: Medium
Pictured: *Lomatium nevadense*

Bluedicks
Dichelostemma capitatum

Other Common Names
Brodiaea, Wild hyacinth

Range & Habitat
Bluedicks is found from Oregon and California, southwest to southern Nevada, southern Utah, much of mid elevation Arizona, and finally to southwest New Mexico. In our area, look to Desert Scrub, Desert Grassland, and Transition regions.

Edible Uses
One of the tastier Lily family plants, Bluedicks is edible from flower and stem to root bulb. The flower and stem are easy to eat when in the field. The bulbs take a little more effort, but they are worth the work. Although they are usually no more than several inches below the ground's surface, consider yourself lucky if found growing in non–rocky and non–hardened soils.

Bluedicks' bulbs are starchy, even to the point of being mucilaginous. Pleasant and mild tasting, they need no preparation aside from washing in a little water. Eaten raw, steamed, or roasted with seasonings in foil, they make for a fine addition to any wild food diet.

Medicinal Uses
There are no medicinal uses for Bluedicks.

Cautions
There are no cautions for Bluedicks.

Special Note
Bluedicks can be confused with a number of Wild onion species (Allium). Usually the two plants do not overlap in range (Wild onion tends to grow at higher elevations). If in doubt, unearth several bulbs. If onion–scented then it is in fact Wild onion.

Sustenance Index: High
Pictured: *Dichelostemma capitatum*

Bowlesia
Bowlesia incana

Other Common Names
Hairy bowlesia

Range & Habitat
This small annual herb is found throughout much of California, southern Nevada, Arizona, New Mexico, and Texas. Its native range also includes parts of Mexico and South America.

In response to abundant winter/spring rains in the Sonoran region, it can cover some grounds like a blanket. Normally though, it is resigned to growing under desert shrubs and trees, and next to rocks and boulders, where it gains protection from the sun.

Edible Uses
Bowlesia is a plain mild–celery tasting edible; however, it is a bit coarse and somewhat hairy. Pick the leaf when young and eat it as is, mix it with other greens in a salad, or eat it as a garnish.

Truth be told, due to Bowlesia's hairiness, it gets a little tiresome eaten alone.

Medicinal Uses
There are no significant medicinal uses for Bowlesia; however, the dried herb does make a pleasant and mild–tasting beverage tea.

Cautions
There are no cautions for Bowlesia eaten in small to moderate amounts. It is conceivable that larger quantities may cause some gastrointestinal irritation due the plant's abundance of leaf and stem hair.

Special Note
Bowlesia is a member of the Carrot family (Apiaceae or Umbelliferae). It is native to the Americas but is now found as a weed in other parts of the world.

Sustenance Index: Low
Pictured: *Bowlesia incana*

Canyon Walnut
Juglans major

Other Common Names
Arizona walnut, Nogal

Range & Habitat
Canyon walnut is found abundantly along waterways and in canyons throughout central and southeastern Arizona.

In New Mexico, it is predominant along the Gila River and southern Rio Grande drainages. The tree is also found in southwestern Texas.

Edible Uses
Although smaller than English and Black walnut, Canyon walnut is just as edible. Gather the walnuts when the outer skin begins to darken or shortly after they fall to the ground. Air dry in a bucket or spread them out on a cardboard flat. Even though this species has a thicker shell and less nutmeat than other walnuts, it's just as tasty.

A tough nut to crack, I like to gradually apply pressure to it using a table–mounted vise as opposed to a strike of a hammer or brick. Whatever method is decided upon – shell and eat them like any other walnut. Like most wild nuts, Canyon walnut is a choice animal food. Once they fall to the ground they do not remain long.

Medicinal Uses, Caution, & Special Note
All Walnut species have therapeutic gastrointestinal tract stimulant/astringent qualities.

There are no cautions for the nut. Like other Walnuts, the bark/leaf/green hull is often touted as a topical/internal anti–fungal/anti–parasitic treatment. Skip it; there are better plant medicines (Barberry or Simaruba family plants) for such issues without the potential of tissue irritation. All parts of the plant (leaf/inner bark/hull) will stain the skin (and fabrics) brown and may cause contact dermatitis (green leaf/green hull) if handled.

Sustenance Index: High
Pictured: *Juglans major*

Catclaw

Acacia greggii

Range & Habitat

Abundant in a number of varying habitats, look for Catclaw in desert valleys, drainage areas, and on hillsides.

Edible Uses

Even though the mature beans are not a choice desert legume, they are nonetheless edible. Collect the beans in the pod while still on the plant once they become ripe and dry. Shuck the beans from the pod. Soak the beans for 24 hours, strain, and add fresh water. This soak/strain process can be repeated *ad nauseam* in order to remove any potential digestive irritants. Cook the beans until soft like any other legume. Eat solo or add them in equal proportions to other bean combinations. The cooked beans can also be dehydrated for future use.

Medicinal Uses

The leaves, like other desert legume shrubs, have mild astringent properties. Use them as a powder or as a wash on cuts and scrapes.

Cautions

Indians thought of Catclaw's beans as a last resort food. The unleached bean was well-known to cause digestive upset and worse if consumed in large amounts. 'Cyanogens' (compounds also found in apple seeds) are reported for the plant. They are toxic if ingested in large amounts. This is not a concern if the beans have first been properly processed (soak/rinse/cook).

Special Note

The beans of other Acacia species can be used like Catclaw. The immature beans (and roots) have a peculiar onion–like/body odor smell. This dissipates (almost entirely) upon drying.

Sustenance Index: Medium
Pictured: *Acacia greggii*

Cattail

Typha spp.

Other Common Names
Punks, Narrowleaf cattail, Southern cattail, Espadilla, Cola de gato

Range & Habitat
A number of Cattail species are common throughout the Southwest. In the Sonoran region, mainly Typha domingensis (Southern cattail) is encountered. Cattail is an aquatic plant. It is found in marshes, swampy areas, and in shallow sections of ponds and lakes.

Edible Uses
Utilized worldwide, Cattail is one of the more significant food plants. The young leafing shoots (2' or under) are collected and used as a potherb, or cooked and added to soups, etc. The inner base core of the young shoot is gathered by peeling back the leaves. It is eaten raw or chopped and added to salads, or steamed/sautéed, etc. The immature flowerheads (punks) are boiled/cooked and eaten (eat around the tough inner stem).

Cattail pollen is collected by banging/shaking the mature punks in a container. Rich in protein, the pollen can be added to other flours in making baked goods (or eaten as a gruel). The post–flowering roots of Cattail are also utilized by cutting away the outer fibrous layers. This leaves a starchy inner core, which can be eaten as is, or cooked and eaten, or dried, ground, and shifted, and utilized as a nutritious flour.

Medicinal Uses
There are no medicinal uses for Cattail.

Cautions & Special Note
Before collecting, be sure that Cattail is growing in a non–contaminated area. Regardless of species, all can be used alike.

Chia

Salvia columbariae

Range & Habitat

Found throughout much of California, low elevation Nevada, southern Utah, Arizona, and New Mexico, Chia is a winter/springtime annual. Responding to seasonal rains, the plant is commonly found on rocky hillsides, slopes, roadsides, and washsides. Where there is one Chia plant, there are usually others close by.

Edible Uses

Chia seeds are collected once the seed heads are dry from mid to late spring. With gloves, crush the seed heads in a slight breeze. This will allow the heavier seeds to drop (into a container) while the crushed seed casings blow away. Like most seeds, Chia's are high in protein and carbohydrates, making them an important sustenance food.

A fortifying mucilaginous gruel is made by soaking Chia seeds overnight in 3–4 parts water. The seeds are also ground and used like other flours in baking, or they are simply moistened with water and shaped into cakes and eaten once dry.

Medicinal Uses

A tincture or tea made from Chia leaf is an aromatic carminative. Use it for the relief of indigestion, gas, and bloating. The tea is gargled for wintertime sore throats or swallowed to retard sweating in cases of long–standing low temperate fevers.

Cautions & Special Note

There are no cautions for the seeds. Closely related Chia sage (Salvia hispanica) was once a very important seed crop for several Mesoamerican cultures. This species is also the main edible Chia seed found in commerce (and the seed used in the well–known 'Chia pet'). Salvia columbariae (profiled) seed is nearly identical in nutritional aspects.

Sustenance Index: High
Pictured: *Salvia columbariae*

Cholla

Cylindropuntia spp.

Other Common Names
Staghorn cholla, Jumping cholla, Cane cholla, Pencil cholla, etc.

Range & Habitat
Distributed across the Southwest, various Cholla species are found from low–elevation alkali flats to mixed Conifer/Oak Woodlands.

Edible Uses
Cholla's immature flower buds are collected before the flowers develop. Later in the season, the fruit are gathered similarly. The thorns and glochids are removed via roasting, boiling, scrubbing, mechanically with a screen, or a combination of techniques (I scrub them with a toothbrush in water). Buds/fruit (w/ or w/o seeds) can then be eaten raw (limited), roasted, or dried for later use. The immature and non–woody joints can also be de–thorned/roasted and eaten.

    A simple recipe after the buds have been de–thorned: wrap them in foil with a little soy or barbecue sauce and roast them on a grill or campfire coals for 15–20 minutes.

Medicinal Uses
The pulp material, like Prickly pear, has blood sugar stabilizing and cholesterol lowering effects. The roots are a soothing diuretic.

Cautions & Special Note
Too much raw material may cause mild fever, chills, and stomach cramps. Small thorns (glochids) can cover much of the plant. Use gloves or tongs when collecting the buds/fruit.

    Most (if not all) Cholla species can be utilized in similar ways. Minor variations in taste and fruit/bud size from species to species should be expected. Cooking/roasting (with seasoning) reduces Cholla's (whatever part) tart–slime qualities.

Sustenance Index: High
Pictured: *Cylindropuntia spinosior* (top) | *Cylindropuntia arbuscula* cooked buds (bottom)

Desert Hackberry

Celtis pallida

Other Common Names

Hackberry bush, Spiny hackberry, Granjeno, Huasteco

Range & Habitat

Desert hackberry is found from southern Arizona, southwestern New Mexico, southern Texas (there is also a small population in western Florida) to points in central Mexico. It is common to lower elevation areas, particularly along draws, gullies, rocky hillsides, and on sandy flats. It is native to both Sonoran and Chihuahuan Deserts.

Edible Uses

Desert hackberry is simply a sweet/ very edible berry that can be consumed as is or collected in mass and prepared as a jam or jelly (a jelly bag will need to be used – the seeds are large).

Some view the crunchy seeds as a mild deterrent to eating, but they can be eaten with no harm along with the berry's flesh.

Medicinal Uses

There are no medicinal uses for Desert hackberry.

Cautions

There are no cautions for Desert hackberry.

Special Note

Providing both food and cover, Desert hackberry is a particular favorite of wildlife. In many areas Hackberry tree (Celtis reticulata) is found near Desert hackberry. This fruit's large seed and small mesocarp (flesh portion) make it a poor food choice.

Sustenance Index: Medium
Pictured: *Celtis pallida*

Desert Hollygrape
Berberis spp. (Mahonia spp.)

Other Common Names
Fremont's barberry, Red barberry, Algerita

Range & Habitat
The majority of Desert hollygrape species (Mahonia fremontii, M. haematocarpa, and M. trifoliolata) are mostly found throughout upper Sonoran, grassland, chaparral, and Juniper–Oak regions.

Edible Uses
Most species of Berberis have sweet–tart (sometimes with a hint of bitter) tasting fruit. Pleasant and refreshing, the berries can be eaten directly from the bush, prepared as a jam/jelly, or dried for later use. Most American Indians in the area utilized the berries as a seasonal–supplemental food.

Medicinal Uses
Root preparations are significantly antimicrobial due to berberine and related alkaloids. The liver/gallbladder and digestive organs are also influenced by the root's internal use. Closely related to Barberry and Oregongrape, Desert hollygrape's medicinal uses are the same.

Cautions
There are no cautions for the fruit.

Special Note
Scientific names for this group of plants can be trying. The old system was simple and made this distinction: if the plant has holly–like spiny leaves, it is a Mahonia (Hollygrape, Oregongrape, etc.); however, if the plant has stem and branch thorns, it is a Berberis (Barberry). Now though, classifiers lump them all into the Berberis genus. Fortunately for edible and medicinal uses, both plants, spiny–leaved or thorny shrub, are used the same.

Sustenance Index: Medium
Pictured: *Berberis trifoliolata* (top) | *Berberis haematocarpa* (bottom)

19

Desert Lily
Hesperocallis undulata

Other Common Names
Ajo lily

Range & Habitat
Desert lily is encountered throughout the low–elevation expanses of western Arizona. Somewhat common (but elusive) to both the Sonoran and Mojave Deserts, look to sandy basins, flats, and slopes. Creosote bush is a notable companion plant.

Edible Uses
The bulbs of Desert lily are generally larger than those of Bluedicks and Mariposa lily, yet of similar flavor and consistency. Starchy and pleasant tasting, simply remove the outer protective 'skin' of each bulb before eating. They are edible raw with no preparation or they can first be roasted or boiled. As a sustaining carbohydrate–rich root 'vegetable' Desert lily is a plant of note.

Medicinal Uses
There are no medicinal uses for Desert lily.

Cautions
There are no cautions for Desert lily.

Special Note
Desert lily joins Mariposa lily and Bluedicks, also Lily family plants, as a bulb–type edible. Botanically affiliated, they all can be treated about the same regarding their uses.

Although Desert lily is a perennial, its above–ground portions are not long–lasting. Its short two to three week window of collection is not due to any lack of bulb material, but rather from a lack of noticeable leaf/flower/stalk growth; once Desert lily flowers and seeds, it diminishes quickly.

Adequate winter rains are important for its above ground growth. During years of winter drought, Desert lily may not sprout and flower at all. Instead, it conserves resources, remaining in a low–activity state until triggered by a future winter rainy season.

Sustenance Index: High
Pictured: *Hesperocallis undulata*   *Photo by Julie Nelson*

Devil's Claw

Proboscidea spp.

Other Common Names
Unicorn plant, Doubleclaw, Cuernitos

Range & Habitat
Various species of Devil's claw are found throughout most of the United States. In the Sonoran Desert and surrounding zones the annual Proboscidea parviflora and perennial P. althaeifolia are the two species encountered. Somewhat common in lower to middle elevations, look to sandy washsides, roadsides, trailsides, and other disturbed soils.

Edible Uses
Gather the young fruit or 'claws' before they become fibrous and woody. Or if further along in the season when the claws have become woody (but still green), snap off the last inch or so of the claw tips and use those. Chop, boil, and rinse the claws/tips to remove the off–smelling surface stickiness. They are not a bad tasting edible if seasoned properly. The young claws also make a fine pickled food.

The mature seeds are also edible. They are ground into a meal and mixed with other flours or moistened and sun–dried as a cake.

The American species with the greatest edible accounting (and range) is Proboscidea louisianica. During the 1800s it was a regional (Great Plains) favorite as a pickled vegetable. One entrepreneurial company even went as far as to brand it 'Pickle of the Plains'.

Medicinal Uses, Cautions, & Special Note
There are no significant medicinal uses for Devil's claw. Besides the repugnant smell, there are no cautions for Devil's claw. The dark fibers from the mature–dried fruit are utilized by Tohono O'odham basket weavers as a black/brown accent.

Sustenance Index: Medium
Pictured: *Proboscidea parviflora* (top) | *Proboscidea althaeifolia* (bottom)

SUMMER FRUIT

Elder
Sambucus spp.

Other Common Names
American black elderberry, Blue elderberry, Mexican elderberry, Saúco

Range & Habitat
Blue/black fruited species of Elder are common throughout North America. Sambucus canadensis is common in the Sonoran region. Look to flood-plains and Mesquite Woodlands or 'bosques' next to washes and other drainages.

Edible Uses
Regardless of species, if the ber-ries are blue/black they are edible. When ripe, the fruit should be sweet or sweetish. On well–hydrated and healthy trees, branches can be so lad-en with fruit that they heavily droop. Great quantities can be gathered in little time.

Eat fresh (limited) or lay out and dry them for future use. Once dry, the berries can be stored or rehydrated/used as needed. Elderberries are a classic jam/jelly base and can be fer-mented instead of grapes to make a wine.

Medicinal Uses
The flowers and leaves have similar uses, with the leaves being about twice as strong as the flowers. Both parts are used to break dry fevers and as diuretics. They also can be used as low–level antivirals during cold and flu season.

Cautions
The seeds (and other parts of Elder) con-tain small amounts of sambucine and cyanogenic glycosides. Although these compounds are toxic in larger amounts, eating moderate amounts of the fresh fruit (with the seed) is not a problem. For the ingestion of larger quantities, the fruit should be heated/dried (which destroys/reduces these compounds) and/or strained of their small seeds.

Sustenance Index: Medium
Pictured: *Sambucus canadensis*

Feather Tree

Lysiloma watsonii

Other Common Names
Littleleaf false tamarind, Desert fern tree

Range & Habitat
Feather tree's native populations are largely found in Mexico. The small tree's northern–most natural occurrence is in the Rincon Mountains, just east of Tucson. On the chain's southern exposure, stable populations exist situated along mid–desert drainages.

Fortunately, Feather tree is easily propagated and has gained traction over the years as a Mesquite–like ornamental. Beyond its native habitat, look for it in and around Tucson and Phoenix. Roadsides, parks, walkways, and other urban/suburban places are common areas for cultivated Feather tree.

Edible Uses
Feather tree ranks somewhere between Catclaw (low) and Paloverde (high) in terms of its palatability. Once the beans are mature (but still green) in mid–summer, they are removed from the pod and boiled/rinsed at least once (twice will be better). Serve them as a cooked green pea.

If allowed to fully dry in the pod (late summer/early fall), the shucked dried beans should be first soaked, strained, and rinsed. With fresh water, simmer the beans, changing the water until they have no poor taste. Like Paloverde, serve them as a cooked bean.

Medicinal Uses & Cautions
The leaves are used as a mild astringent. The undercooked/poorly leached beans likely have some anti–nutrient qualities (like Catclaw). Before consuming any significant amount, be sure that they are properly processed (soak/rinse/cook), else gastrointestinal upset is likely.

Sustenance Index: High
Pictured: *Lysiloma watsonii*

Flameflower

Phemeranthus aurantiacus

Other Common Names
Orange flameflower

Range & Habitat
Found throughout southern Arizona, New Mexico, and southern/central Texas, Flameflower is common to mid–desert and grassland regions. It is especially abundant on slopes and hillsides, often growing next to larger nurse shrubs or around rocks and boulders.

Edible Uses
Like most Purslane family plants, the entire above ground portion is succulent, certainly edible, and mildly tart tasting. Consumed fresh or cooked, the herbage needs little processing.

Once considered an important food to local Indians, Flameflower's tuberous roots are also edible. They are fair and mild tasting and need little preparation aside from peeling away the root's outer layer. However, if eating more than one or two roots I suggest boiling or steaming them first, then seasoning the cooked root, as quantities of the fresh root can be mildly acrid (depending on season) and a bit fibrous.

For a description of the closely related plant, Talinum paniculatum, see Jewels of opar.

Medicinal Uses
There are no medicinal uses for Flameflower.

Cautions & Special Note
Like most plants in the Purslane family, Flameflower herbage contains its fair share of oxalates. If eating large quantities, be sure to first boil the leaves.

There are a handful of other Phemeranthus species found in the Southwest; their above–ground portions can be used like Flameflower's.

Sustenance Index: Medium
Pictured: *Phemeranthus aurantiacus*

Graythorn

Ziziphus obtusifolia var. canescens

Other Common Names
Lotebush

Range & Habitat
Graythorn's core range is throughout the low to mid Sonoran Desert. From rocky slopes and hillsides to expansive flats, the plant is abundant. Companion plants are Desert hackberry, Saguaro, and Wolfberry.

Edible Uses
When ripe and hydrated, the purple–black berries are very sweet. However, not all specimens provide pleasant–tasting fruit, even when ripe. Possible hydration or soil factors contribute to the fruit's palatability. If they are poor tasting, simply move on to a better group of plants.

    Eat the berries freely when fresh. They too can be dried for later use. Graythorn fruit also serves as a good base for jams and jellies. A sweet syrup can be produced by making a strong dried fruit tea: strain and reduce it to a syrup consistency by prolonged low–heat simmering.

Medicinal Uses
There are no significant medicinal uses for Graythorn.

Cautions
There are no special cautions for Graythorn.

Special Note
Eurasian native, Jujube (Ziziphus jujuba), is a close relative of Graythorn. In that part of the world it is an important fruit crop, where it is eaten raw, dried, or made into a jam or jelly. Also Traditional Chinese Medicine assigns minor medicinal qualities to Jujube fruit.

Sustenance Index: Medium
Pictured: *Ziziphus obtusifolia var. canescens*

Ground Cherry
Physalis spp.

Other Common Names
Tomatillo, Husk tomato

Range & Habitat
Ground cherry is both an Old and New World plant. California, Arizona, New Mexico, Texas, and adjacent southern states host the most species in America. In the Sonoran region look to an array of habitats: from shrub–shaded draws to open flats and hillsides.

    The plant can be unpredictable to find. Once a group is located, remember its location for future reference.

Edible Uses
Usually ripening from late summer to fall, each fruit is encased in an inflated sac. Depending on species, the fruit are greenish–tan to yellowish–orange (occasionally darker) when ripe. Be sure to remove the 'cherry' from its encasement before eating. They taste sweetish–acidic and tomato–like. If immature, they are better cooked. When ripe, eat raw or combine them with other wild edibles. Ground cherry salsa is a local favorite (substitute Ground cherry for tomatoes). It is one of the better tasting nightshades we have in the region.

Medicinal Uses
Like other nightshades, the foliage is potentially drying to the gastrointestinal tract and ocular/nasal regions.

Cautions
There are no cautions for the fruit. Ground cherry's foliage is medicinal (or toxic in larger amounts). Some may confuse Horse nettle (Solanum elaeagnifolium) in appearance with Ground cherry. Unlike Ground cherry, Horse nettle's fruit have no encasing and are yellow. Horse nettle fruit are not edible.

Sustenance Index: Medium
Pictured: *Physalis hederifolia*

Hedgehog Cactus

Echinocereus engelmannii

Other Common Names
Engelmann's hedgehog

Range & Habitat
Hedgehog is fairly common through-out the desert elevations of the west-ern half of Arizona. Southern Califor-nia, Nevada, and Utah also host the cactus.

Edible Uses
The fruit is the most reliably edible part: the inner pulp is pleasantly sour–sweet and very palatable. Sim-ply slice the fruit in half, scoop out the pulp and small crunchy seeds, and consume raw. The inner fruit material can also be dried for later use, or pre-pared as a jam or jelly.

    The inner stem material of Hedgehog can also be eaten. More of a survival food, and best boiled or roasted first, the inner stem tastes much like Prickly pear pad. Simply chop the top from a section, then carve down the sides to remove the thorns. Cut this now cactus–cube from its base; eat raw in limited amounts, or cook to eat in larger quantities.

Medicinal Uses
The inner stem, like Prickly pear, has sooth-ing topical qualities (apply it to sunburn and burns). Internally, it has potential to lower blood sugar and cholesterol levels.

Cautions & Special Note
There are no cautions for the fruit (besides navigating the thorns); however, between rodents eating the fruit and poor development, the ripe fruit can be hard to find. Be sure to cook the inner stem if eating it in significant quantities: see 'Cactus fever' under Prickly pear. Many states list various species of Hedge-hog as a protected plant. Try to find a sizable population before utilizing the limb material.

Sustenance Index: High
Pictured: *Echinocereus engelmannii*

Horse Purslane
Trianthema portulacastrum

Other Common Names
Desert horse purslane, Pigweed

Range & Habitat
Mostly a plant of the low and mid deserts, look for Horse purslane in disturbed soils.

Vacant lots, field edges, backyards, and walkway sides are reliable places for this annual. It quickly carpets large areas in response to abundant summer rains.

Edible Uses
Treat Horse purslane like true Purslane (Portulaca oleracea) in regard to its edibility. Succulent, hydrated, and mildly sour, the newer young leaves are the choice part. Consume them as is, as a salad ingredient, or even as a lettuce substitute in a sandwich.

Briefly sautéed (like bean sprouts), they add a pleasing tart–quality to a stir–fry or any dish that calls for such a taste.

Medicinal Uses
A freshly bruised poultice applied to swellings will be found drawing and antiinflammatory.

Cautions
Horse purslane is high in calcium oxalate, which can be irritating to the urinary tract (and pro–kidney stone development) if ingested in sufficient quantities. As an occasional edible or salad addition there is little to fear; however, if consumed every day while in season (fresh) it may be problematic for some individuals.

Special Note
Compared to Purslane, Horse purslane's leaves are larger but thinner. It has small red flowers (Purslane's are yellow) and is more aggressive and abundant in growth than Purslane.

Sustenance Index: Low
Pictured: *Trianthema portulacastrum*

Ironwood
Olneya tesota

Other Common Names
Desert ironwood, Palo fierro

Range & Habitat
Like Saguaro, Ironwood is a Sonoran Desert indicator. From south/central Arizona to southeastern California, look to low elevation habitats: basins, valleys, expansive flats, and along drainage areas. Paloverde is a common companion tree.

Edible Uses
Ironwood beans were one of the main vegetable food sources for all Indian tribes living in its proximity. The bean is easy to collect (when in season), high in protein, and needs very little preparation.

    Early in the season, the immature beans (with pods) are gathered and boiled once or twice and served as a wild pea pod of sorts. They are astringent at this point (but not bitter), so boiling and rinsing are important. Further along in the season, the beans (still green) are removed from the pod and eaten raw. They are mild and pleasant tasting (slightly astringent) and are eaten freely, added to salads, etc., or cooked like sweet peas.

    Early to mid–summer the dried bean is collected, removed from the pod, and eaten as is: they are crunchy–chewy at this point and are not astringent. They also can be prepared like any other seed/bean – soak, rinse, and simmer until soft.

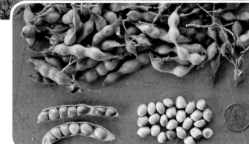

Medicinal Uses, Cautions & Special Note
Aside from the leaves (and other parts) being astringent, there are no significant medicinal uses for Ironwood. Indians once prized Ironwood for its dense wood. Bows, handles, and other wooden creations were made from its sturdy limbs and trunks. Today, many woodworking artisans can still be found using Ironwood as a base material.

Sustenance Index: High
Pictured: *Olneya tesota*

Jewels of Opar
Talinum paniculatum

Other Common Names
Rama de sapo, Pink baby's breath

Range & Habitat
Jewels of opar's main area is south–southeastern Arizona. Look to rocky slopes, mid–mountain foothills, and Desert Grassland regions. Hidalgo County New Mexico hosts the plant, as does the gulf region of Texas. It too is found throughout a number of southeastern states.

Edible Uses
Consider Jewels of opar like Purslane or Flameflower, but on steroids. Its leaves are massive compared to these others, but they all taste about the same – succulent and tart.

If eating daily Jewels of opar leaf salads (this is possible in the late summer when at its peak from the monsoons) go easy on it, or boil/rinse it first, due to the oxalates (most tart/sour plants taste that way due to oxalates).

Also, similar to Purslane is its nutritional profile. The leaf is high in omega–3 essential fatty acids, calcium, magnesium, potassium, and vitamins A and C.

The roots are also edible, and taste about the same as Flameflower's – bland and sometimes fibrous.

Medicinal Uses
There are no significant medicinal uses for Jewels of opar.

Cautions
Oxalate leaf content: boil the leaves first if consuming in large quantities. Kidney stones suffers should generally forgo eating large amounts of the fresh leaf.

Sustenance Index: Low
Pictured: *Talinum paniculatum* (top) | *Talinum paniculatum* leaf vs. Purslane (bottom)

Jojoba
Simmondsia chilensis

Other Common Names
Goatnut, Deernut

Range & Habitat
From central/southern Arizona, southern/central Utah, to southern California, look for Jojoba at low to mid elevations. The bush exists in nearly pure stands in many parts of Arizona. It is often a dominant hillside grower.

Edible Uses
Jojoba 'nuts' should be gathered when they are mature (dark brown). After removing the seed from the husk, limited quantities can be eaten raw, but really, they should be parched/roasted for 30–40 minutes at 300–350 degrees in order to tame the seed's nearly indigestible wax.

If 5 raw seeds can be eaten without indigestion, after roasting maybe 10 can be consumed. It's a difficult wild food to digest in moderate to large amounts. A strong decoction of the roasted seed is imbibed as a coffee–like substitute.

Medicinal Uses
Jojoba leaves are very astringent. A strong leaf tea is applied as a wash to cuts, scrapes, and burns.

Cautions
Eating too many seeds will cause gastrointestinal upset. It can be assumed that the seeds have some anti–nutrient qualities.

Special Note
During the 70s there was a popular movement to grow Jojoba for the seed's oily wax. This wax was seen by entrepreneurial growers as a potential industrial lubricant, possibly rivaling petroleum–based oils in application. It never did catch on, but remnant Jojoba fields can still be seen in western AZ. Jojoba's oily wax does have a following as a natural cosmetic.

Sustenance Index: Low
Pictured: *Simmondsia chilensis*

Lambsquarters

Chenopodium spp.

Other Common Names
Goosefoot, Quelites

Range & Habitat
Species of Lambsquarters are composed of both native and non–native plants. In the Sonoran Desert (and surrounding parts) the majority of plants do well in disturbed soils: roadsides, trailsides, cattle tank areas, etc.

Edible Uses
The plant's young leaves are the most palatable part. With age, the leaves may become a little acrid. For the consumption of moderate to large quantities, the leaves should be first boiled and then rinsed. Most species are also very high in calcium and vitamin A.

The seeds of Lambsquarters too are a good food source. They are gathered and winnowed once the plant starts to bolt; after which they are ground into a meal or simply added to and/or cooked with other foods.

Medicinal Uses
Epazote (Chenopodium ambrosioides) is the main medicinal species of the genus. Really not a food plant per se, it is more of a spice and useful carminative. Epazote also smells and tastes differently than Lambsquarters: when crushed fresh, like restroom disinfectant.

Cautions & Special Note
Kidney stone suffers may find that eating the fresh plant (daily) will contribute to this condition (due to a high oxalate content). There is no problem with Lambsquarters as an occasional edible.

Chenopodium album is the main Lambsquarters species, though it is not often found in the desert. C. berlandieri and C. fremontii are two more abundant regional species with identical edible uses. Lambsquarters' notable reflective/sparkle quality, visible especially on the leaves' surfaces, is due to calcium deposition.

Sustenance Index: Medium
Pictured: *Chenopodium spp.*

Lemonade Berry

Rhus aromatica (Rhus trilobata)

Other Common Names
Skunkbush, Squawbush, Sumac skunkbush, Threeleaf sumac

Range & Habitat
A wide ranging southwestern/western shrub, look for Lemonade berry on mid–mountain and foothill scrub–covered hillsides just above desert elevations.

Edible Uses
Lemonade berry's ripe fruit are red, sticky, and lemon–sour tasting. Once gathered, a pleasantly tart and refreshing tea can be made from the fruit. This process, whether a sun–tea or a hot water infusion, is Lemonade berry's best preparation. The sun tea is an easy enough process: infuse 1oz of berries in 1qt of water. Let the mixture stand for at least several hours, then strain and sweeten the tea to taste.

Although not Lemonade berry's best use, the fruit can simply be eaten as is (better sucked on and then spit out) – they are mealy and dry.

Medicinal Uses
The leaves are astringent and can be used as a soothing poultice for burns, scrapes, and abrasions.

Cautions
There are no cautions for Lemonade berry.

Special Note
All other red–fruited Rhus species can be used like Lemonade berry. The fruit of most species also contain small amounts of vitamin C – approximately 2–3mgs per ounce. Related Poison ivy/Poison sumac have a white–milky sap when a stem or leaf is broken (Lemonade berry has no milky sap). Also, unlike the red fruit of Lemonade berry, Poison ivy and Poison sumac have cream–greenish colored fruit.

Sustenance Index: Low
Pictured: *Rhus aromatica*

London Rocket
Sisymbrium irio

Other Common Names
Wild mustard, Winter cress

Range & Habitat
Originally native to Eurasia, London rocket is now found worldwide. It has a significant range throughout the Southwest. It is usually found around waste areas, roadsides, ditches, and generally where the ground has been disturbed.

Edible Uses
London rocket is one of our better tasting mustards. A little spicier than Watercress, the young leaves and flowerheads make a great addition to salads or stir–fries. It is not a sub-sistence food, but more of an accent.

Medicinal Uses
London rocket is stimulating to diges-tion. A paste of the freshly crushed seeds (like most other Mustards) can also be used topically as a mild count-er–irritant for the temporary relief of chronic aches and pains.

Cautions
Eating too much fresh London rocket may cause kidney sensitivity, and in some women, stimulant menses.

Special Note
Even though most Mustard family plants are edible and have mustard tastes, unlike London rocket, many will be bitter or too tough to eat consistently.

London rocket is related to the bet-ter–known garden vegetables Broccoli, Cauliflower, Kale, and of course Mustard greens (Brassica or Sinapis).

Sustenance Index: Low
Pictured: *Sisymbrium irio*

Mallow

Malva neglecta and M. parviflora

Other Common Names
Common mallow, Cheeseweed mallow, High mallow

Range & Habitat
A non–native genus that exists seasonally in vast tracts (farmland/vacant lots) throughout Arizona, Mallow responds most consistently to summer rains. Look for it along field edges, fallow fields, roadsides, ditches, and similarly disturbed soils.

Malva parviflora is the lower elevation grower. It is very common in and around the Tucson and Phoenix areas. M. neglecta is typical found higher in elevation – Flagstaff, etc. Both are nearly identical in appearance and uses.

Edible Uses
The leaves are the most palatable part of Mallow. Collected while young they are combined with other greens and eaten raw, added to soups, or simply cooked like spinach. They will be a little mucilaginous/slimy (Mallow is related to Okra), but still pleasant tasting and nutritious.

Although the leaf tea does have some medicinal application, it is mild enough to be used as a beverage tea.

Medicinal Uses & Cautions
Both the leaves and roots make a soothing tea for sore throats and coughs. The crushed fresh leaf poultice also makes a fine topical treatment for burns, rashes, scrapes, minor stings, and other similar afflictions. There are no cautions for Mallow.

Special Note
Although non–toxic, other desert Mallow family plants (Globemallow, Desert hibiscus, and Indian mallow) do not have the same palatability as Mallow.

Sustenance Index: Low
Pictured: *Malva neglecta*

Mariposa Lily

Calochortus kennedyi

Other Common Names
Desert mariposa lily

Range & Habitat
The epicenter of the genus is California, where dozens of species exist.
The most common plant in the Sonoran Desert is Calochortus kennedyi. Abundant in mid to upper desert
regions, look for it on hillsides, slopes,
and rock–strewn slopes.

Edible Uses
From flower and stem to root bulb,
the whole plant is edible. The flowers (and stems/leaves) can be eaten
without killing the plant. They are
pleasant tasting and have a mild nut-
ty flavor.

   The root bulbs require more effort to procure. They are often ½' or
so beneath the ground's surface, so
digging with a trowel will be necessary. The bulbs provide more sustenance due to their greater carbohydrate content. They too are pleasant
tasting and starchy. Eat them raw or
cooked.

   As for other Calochortus species, I have not sampled everyone;
however, for the ones that I have tried,
they are all similar in edibility and taste.

Medicinal Uses
Mariposa lily has no medicinal use.

Cautions
There are no cautions for Mariposa lily.

Special Note
Be sure the species at hand is abundant, for a number of them are listed as threatened or endan-
gered. The plant is only identifiable for 2–4 weeks during mid–spring, when it is in flower/seed.
After this window has passed, its above–ground trace is gone until next year.

Sustenance Index: High
Pictured: *Calochortus kennedyi*

Mesquite

Prosopis spp.

Other Common Names
Velvet mesquite, Honey mesquite, Screwbean mesquite

Range & Habitat
Somewhat diverse in habitat, various species of Mesquite are found throughout grassland, desert, and scrub regions. Drainages, hillsides, and flats are common growing areas.

Edible Uses
Unlike the majority of Pea family edible plants, it is the pod and not the seed of Mesquite that is considered the main food.

Before ripening fully, when the pods are green, they are chewed for their natural sugars. After the pods have fully ripened and are dry and brittle, they are ground into a coarse flour. The flour is very sweet to bland tasting (depending on species) and is eaten alone or used as a baking base. Primitive cakes are made by forming the flour with a little water. They are then dried in the sun. The pod flour combines well with other flours in baking (cookies, bread, etc.). A surprisingly sweet syrup can also be made by boiling down a tea of the pods until the desired consistency is obtained.

Medicinal Uses, Cautions, & Special Note
The pods are stabilizing to blood sugar levels. Hardened sap nodules are sucked on for the relief of gastritis/heartburn, or made into a weak eyewash for eye inflammation. There are no cautions for Mesquite.

Technically, any species of Mesquite is edible; however, Velvet mesquite (Prosopis velutina) is generally considered to produce the sweetest (and most abundant) pods. Try to collect the pods while on the tree – they mold quickly after falling to the ground. When grinding the pods, the seed too can be included.

Sustenance Index: High
Pictured: *Prosopis velutina*

Miner's Lettuce

Claytonia perfoliata

Other Common Names
Indian lettuce, Winter purslane, Spring beauty

Range & Habitat
From Alaska to California, east to South Dakota, Colorado, Arizona, and New Mexico, Miner's lettuce needs shady and damp soils to thrive. In early spring look for the plant next to rocks and boulders where the soil is protected from the sun.

Edible Uses
Like Purslane, Flameflower, and Jewels of opar (same family), all parts of Miner's lettuce are edible. Mildly tart and succulent, it is one of the most refreshing wild edibles we have in Arizona. Eat it as is or add the plant to salads or use it as a garnish. Although still edible, once cooked/boiled Miner's lettuce loses much of its taste and body.

Medicinal Uses
There are no medicinal uses for Miner's lettuce.

Cautions
If eating large amounts everyday, a quick water boil of the leaf should first be employed. Compounds (oxalates), common to most Purslane family plants, can irritate the kidneys (kidney stone suffers may want to eat Miner's lettuce sparingly).

Special Note
Other Claytonia species are just as edible, though no other species is as abundant as Miner's lettuce in the Sonoran region. For instance, Claytonia virginica (Spring beauty) is the main edible species for the eastern part of the country. Unlike Miner's lettuce though, it is a perennial and has larger edible roots.

Sustenance Index: Low
Pictured: *Claytonia perfoliata*

Monkey Flower
Mimulus guttatus

Other Common Names
Yellow monkey flower, Common monkey flower, Seep monkey flower

Range & Habitat
A wide–ranging western species, look for this plant along streams and springs in the Sonoran region, as well as low to mid elevation peripheral areas.

Edible Uses
Monkey flower makes for a fair–tasting early springtime green. The young leaves, before the plant's stalk and flowers develop, are the best edible part. At this time, they can be eaten raw, or boiled/steamed and eaten as a cooked green. The taste is like mildly bitter lettuce.

Further along in the season, when Monkey flower becomes a mature plant, it can still be eaten raw, but it is often too bitter to be consumed in any quantity. Boiling the leaf, then following up with a quick rinse will remove some of the bitterness allowing greater amounts to be eaten.

Medicinal Uses
There are no medicinal uses for Monkey flower.

Cautions
There are no cautions for Monkey flower.

Special Note
Monkey flower may be confused with Watercress when young and not in flower. Taste a leaf – if bland yet a little bitter, it is Monkey flower; if mustard–spicy, then it is Watercress.

Sustenance Index: Low
Pictured: *Mimulus guttatus*

New Mexico Thistle
Cirsium neomexicanum

Other Common Names
Thistle, Lavender thistle

Range & Habitat
New Mexico thistle is common throughout the low–mid elevation Southwest. In Arizona, look to desert regions next to fields, ditches, and embankments, and on rocky hillsides and flats.

Edible Uses
Before the flowering stalks emerge, dig the taproots of young first year plants. Cold season/early spring roots will be best. As the plant matures and develops a stalk, the roots quickly become fibrous and woody.

    The young taproots are surprisingly tasty. Crisp and crunchy, with an almost nutty flavor, they are not fibrous or bitter (unlike Wild carrot roots). They are fine raw, but can also be chopped and cooked as an addition to stews and soups.

    Due to New Mexico thistle's ubiquity and abundance, I believe it deserves a higher ranking as an important edible.

Medicinal Uses
There are no significant medicinal uses for New Mexico thistle. The plant is unrelated in use to the popular Milk thistle (Silybum marianum).

Cautions
There are no cautions for New Mexico thistle.

Special Note
New Mexico thistle's stalks are too fibrous to be utilized for food. Other species of Thistle that are taller–faster growing, have more palatable stems.

Sustenance Index: High
Pictured: *Cirsium neomexicanum*

Paloverde
Parkinsonia microphylla

Other Common Names
Littleleaf paloverde, Foothills paloverde, Yellow paloverde

Range & Habitat
Often found with Ironwood and Saguaro, Paloverde's core range is south/western Arizona to southeastern California. A common lower elevation grower, look to expansive flats, foothills, and rocky hillsides.

Edible Uses
As our most edible Paloverde, the fresh beans (still green) are removed from the pods and eaten raw (or boiled like sweet peas). They are pleasant tasting and need little preparation.

After the bean is fully dry (brown in the pod), remove them from the pod and soak/strain and simmer like any other dried bean. The mature beans can also be roasted in an oven and/or ground into a meal or flour and used appropriately.

Medicinal Uses
Aside from the leaves being mildly astringent, there are no medicinal uses for Paloverde.

Cautions
Cookfire/campfire smoke from Paloverde wood is an irritant (more irritating than other woodsmokes).

Special Note
Blue paloverde (Parkinsonia florida) has bitter–tasting beans. Whether gathered green or dried, they will need multiple soaking/rinsing rounds to remove their poor taste. Mexican paloverde (Parkinsonia aculeata), less abundant than the two other species, has very good tasting beans. Like Parkinsonia microphylla, remove the bean from the pod and eat them raw/green. They too are gathered when dry, still hanging from the tree; shuck/soak/rinse/cook as needed.

Sustenance Index: High

Pictured: *Parkinsonia microphylla*

Pápalo

Porophyllum ruderale ssp. macrocephalum

Other Common Names

Papaloquelite, Mata piojo, Yerba porosa, Poreleaf

Range & Habitat

Mexico and points south constitutes Pápalo's core range. North of the border, southeastern Arizona likely hosts the greatest native concentration of the plant. It is also found in southern New Mexico and West Texas – mainly in isolated stands. Mid–mountain rocky slopes and hillsides are usually places for Pápalo.

Edible Uses

Pápalo has a long history of culinary use. Its addition to food as an accent or spice predates Columbus' arrival in the Americas. Even the name Pápalo is a derivative of the Nahuatl word for butterfly (all Porophyllums are common moth–butterfly feeding plants).

Use Pápalo as a food spice – like fresh Cilantro or Basil (Pápalo is sometimes referred to as tasting like Cilantro). It's just too aromatic and powerful to be eaten alone. Also, it's best to use the fresh herb. Cooking removes nearly all of its interesting flavor qualities.

After the monsoons have started in the summer, begin looking for the plant (it's an annual). Once found, crush and smell the leaf – it should be strongly aromatic. Collect just the larger healthy leaves – the stems have little aroma and are fibrous.

Medicinal Uses & Cautions

Like any Porophyllum, if a small handful of Pápalo is eaten, its medicinal attributes should become evident. Stomach bloating and indigestion are remedied, which is another reason why the plant's a traditional spice – it settles the stomach. There are no cautions for the culinary use of Pápalo.

Sustenance Index: Low
Pictured: *Porophyllum ruderale ssp. macrocephalum*

Pellitory
Parietaria hespera

Other Common Names
Rillita pellitory, Western pellitory

Range & Habitat
Pellitory is found from Arizona west to southern California. In Arizona it tends to do well in low to mid elevation sheltered areas. Next to boulders, in rock crevices, and under shade–providing shrubs and trees are common places for Pellitory.

Typically an early spring plant, it bolts quickly as temperatures rise. It often is found side–by–side Bowlesia.

Edible Uses
The whole plant is edible. It's a little hairy, but nevertheless, makes a nice addition to salads, or it is simply eaten when encountered. Its taste is distinctly cucumber–like.

Medicinal Uses
There are no medicinal uses for Pellitory.

Cautions
There are no cautions for Pellitory's use.

Special Note
Pellitory is in the Nettle family (Urticaceae). Its closest useful relative is Parietaria officinalis or Pellitory–of–the–wall, a European native often used medicinally like Nettle (Urtica dioica). Both Pellitory–of–the–wall and Nettle are useful in treating acidic conditions such as gout and urate–type kidney stones/deposits. They also are fair–tasting and can be used as simple beverage teas.

Sustenance Index: Low
Pictured: *Parietaria hespera*

Pincushion Cactus

Mammillaria grahamii

Other Common Names
Fishhook cactus, Globe cactus

Range & Habitat
Supported by both Sonoran and Chihuahuan Deserts, Pincushion cactus is fairly common throughout low to mid elevation Arizona (it doesn't grow much higher than 4000'). It too can be found in southern New Mexico. The edge of its range is West Texas and San Bernardino County, California.

As far as specific habitat is concerned, Pincushion cactus is varied. It's found on rocky slopes, hillsides, basins, and flats, and almost always sheltered by larger shrubs or rocks.

Edible Uses
When ripe, Pincushion cactus fruit appears like a small fresh chili pepper. However, they are not spicy, but mildly tart tasting.

Their best preparation is none: eat them as a fresh edible when encountered in the desert. The fruit's seeds are small enough to be eaten along with the fruit's flesh with no problem.

The chopped fresh fruit has good potential as a salsa ingredient or simply as a salad addition.

Medicinal Uses & Cautions
There are no medicinal uses or cautions for the fruit.

Special Note
Pincushion cactus is on most federal/state watch lists. Like Ocotillo (also protected status), it is very common throughout Arizona. Picking the fruit is not a problem; digging the cactus to transplant into a garden may be.

Pincushion cactus is smaller than Hedgehog cactus. The fruit are very different: one is narrow, tapering, and tart with no thorns. The other is ovoid, very thorny, and sweet.

Poreleaf
Porophyllum gracile

Other Common Names
Slender poreleaf, Odora, Yerba del venado, Deerweed

Range & Habitat
From southern California, Nevada, Utah, to much of Arizona, southern New Mexico and a couple of isolated stands in Texas, Porophyllum gracile is the widest ranging of the Porophyllum group. Look to hillsides, slopes, and flats with related Desert Scrub plant life.

Edible Uses
Best used as a garnish, add fresh Poreleaf leaves to salads and potherb combinations. Having a unique taste and smell, Poreleaf quickly loses its culinary characteristics once dried or cooked. It ranks with Chinchweed as an unknown spice plant, and is always a pleasure to come across in the desert.

Medicinal Uses
The plant's unique pungency (and related physiological effect) is why it is so useful as a culinary accent and stomachic medicine. Nibble on a small handful of leaves for indigestion and bloating.

Cautions
There are no cautions for Poreleaf.

Special Note
Porophyllum ruderale ssp. macrocephalum or Pápalo, also a Poreleaf, has identical uses and is even more palatable than this plant. See P. 42.

Sustenance Index: Low
Pictured: *Porophyllum gracile*

45

Prickly Pear

Opuntia spp.

Other Common Names
Nopal, Tunas, Nopalitos

Range & Habitat
Excluding the extreme Northeast, various Prickly pear species are found throughout the continental United States. In the Arizona deserts Opuntia engelmannii and O. phaeacantha are regionally common.

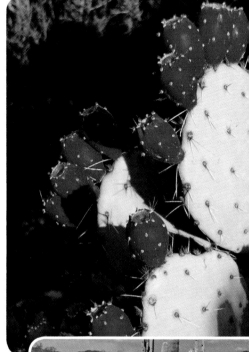

Edible Uses
All species of Prickly pear have edible, sweet (more–or–less), and seed–filled fruit. The flesh is the best portion, but the seeds can be eaten as well. To eat raw, simply slice the fruit open when ripe and scoop out the inner flesh (with seeds) and consume as is. Be sure to not eat the fruit skin due to the abundance of tiny thorns (glochids). The fruit also serves as a good jelly, jam, or juice base.

The young pads (Nopalitos) can also be eaten raw in limited quantities; if cooked, then in larger amounts. They have the taste of a slimy bell pepper. As a cooked vegetable, they are traditionally served with eggs for breakfast. Be sure to first remove the thorns and glochids. The pads can also be pickled.

Medicinal Uses, Cautions & Special Note
Like Aloe vera, the inner pad is soothing to burns, scrapes, and stings. Internally all parts will lower blood sugar and cholesterol levels.

Excessive raw fruit consumption may cause digestive upset. Too much raw pad may cause fever, chills, and digestive upset, collectively known as 'Cactus fever'.

Before using Prickly pear, be sure to remove thorns (and glochids). Mission prickly pear (Opuntia ficus–indica) is found as an ornamental throughout warmer parts of the Southwest. It's the main source of store bought Nopalitos. This species has no to few thorns.

Sustenance Index: High
Pictured: *Opuntia engelmannii*

Purslane
Portulaca oleracea

Other common names
Common purslane, Little hogweed, Verdolaga

Range & habitat
Purslane is predictable in its habitat. Disturbed soils such as vacant lots, walkway edges, and trail and dirt road sides are a few common areas for the plant.

Edible uses
Like most other plants of the same genus, all parts of Purslane are edible. The young leaves and stems are the best tasting. They are pleasantly sour and succulent in consistency. Purslane is best eaten raw, as cooking diminishes its flavor and substance.

Similar to others in the Purslane family, the plant is nutritious. It is high in omega–3 essential fatty acids, calcium, magnesium, potassium and vitamins C and A.

Medicinal uses
There are no medicinal uses for Purslane.

Cautions
Small to moderate amounts of Purslane are fine consumed raw; however, if large amounts are being eaten on a regular basis I suggest quickly boiling and rinsing the plant first. This removes much of the leaves' oxalate content.

Special note
Flameflower, Jewels of opar, and Miner's lettuce are related to Purslane. These plants are in the Purslane family (or according to some botanists, belonging to separate yet related families). They all have edible foliage and (if perennial) edible roots (Purslane is an annual, and therefore has an insignificant root).

Sustenance Index: Low
Pictured: *Portulaca oleracea*

Saguaro
Carnegiea gigantea

Other Common Names
Giant cactus

Range & Habitat
A true Sonoran Desert indicator, Saguaro is found only in central/southern Arizona and in a small region of southeastern California. Ironwood and Paloverde are two common associate trees, also with edible uses.

Edible Uses
Saguaro is rated by some to have the best–tasting fruit of the Sonoran Desert cacti. Fig–like in taste and consistency, its sweetness is more refined than Prickly pear and has none of the subtle tang of Hedgehog. Late June to early July is Saguaro's collecting time. Using a long stick, pole, or even an old Saguaro rib (I use a pool skimmer pole), gently push the fruit from the cactus' growth tip. Gather the fallen fruit and split them open with a knife. The internal fruit/seed material is then scooped out and eaten or prepared as a jam, jelly, drink (alcoholic and otherwise), or even dried in sheets as 'fruit jerky'.

Medicinal Uses & Cautions
There are no medicinal uses for the fruit. Saguaro's small thorns and glochids are weaker than Prickly pear's and Cholla's, but they still can be irritating if rubbed into the mouth or eyes. I recommend wearing gloves while gathering the fruit.

Special Note
An indicator of ripe fruit will be noticeable bird–feeding activity (often Gila woodpeckers) and the fruit just starting to split open. Fruit collection was a major activity for the Tohono O'odham whom once considered this cactus an important supplemental food. Check local regulations before collecting Saguaro fruit on public lands – there may be some red tape to hurdle in order to legally collect the fruit.

Sustenance Index: High
Pictured: *Carnegiea gigantea*

Sow Thistle
Sonchus spp.

Other Common Names
Common sow thistle, Spiny sow thistle

Range & Habitat
A weedy non–native annual, look for Sow thistle in moistened–disturbed soils and around rocky draws that run with intermittent water. Wild lettuce, a plant that is similar in appearance, botanical relation, and edible use, is often found growing near Sow thistle.

Edible Uses
Collect Sow thistle's young leaves when the plant first emerges as a basal rosette in the spring. They are best cooked: boiling, sautéing, or steaming will soften the leaf spines on at least one species (Sonchus asper). Boiling and rinsing the leaves with fresh water will lessen their bitterness.

Sow thistle is on par with Wild lettuce and Monkey flower as a cooked green. It may not be the best wild edible, but it works well to round out some of the better tasting cacti fruit and legumes.

Medicinal Uses
Sow thistle leaf tea is sometimes used as a Dandelion substitute.

Cautions
There are no cautions for Sow thistle.

Special Note
Like Dandelion and Wild lettuce, Sow thistle has a milky sap when a leaf is broken.

Sustenance Index: Low
Pictured: *Sonchus oleraceus* (top) | *Sonchus asper* (bottom)

Texas Mulberry

Morus microphylla

Other Common Names

Wild mulberry, Littleleaf mulberry, Mora wood

Range & Habitat

Fairly common to mid–elevation canyons and drainages, Texas mulberry is found throughout much of Arizona to New Mexico and Texas. Its preferred elevation takes it out of the Sonoran Desert proper, but its association is well–founded, growing in the mountain ranges that rise from the desert's floor.

Edible Uses

The fruit, although smaller than Red and White mulberry, are nearly as sweet and juicy. For a simple foraging treat, eat them freely when encountered in the spring. The fruit also makes an excellent base for jam and jelly preparations.

The purple fruit have the highest anthocyanin content – health–promoting antioxidant pigments. They are also a fair source of potassium and vitamin C.

Medicinal Uses

There are no significant medicinal uses for Texas mulberry.

Cautions

There are no cautions for Texas mulberry.

Special Note

Once upon a time, Texas mulberry branches and wood were considered a regional orange dye source.

White mulberry (Morus alba) can occasionally be found as a planted ornamental throughout Arizona. It grows to be a medium–sized tree and was once sought after as a shade (and fruit) provider.

Sustenance Index: Medium
Pictured: *Morus microphylla*

Tumbleweed

Salsola tragus

Other Common Names
Russian thistle

Range & Habitat
Most Salsola species are native to Siberia/Russia/Central Asia, but thrive as invasive weeds throughout the West. As in other arid regions, a number of Tumbleweed species (especially Salsola tragus) does well in the Southwest and Sonoran regions. Look to disturbed soils: road and trail sides, vacant lots, and fallow fields.

Edible Uses
The young leafing tips of Tumbleweed's spring growth are edible. They are eaten raw or steamed/boiled and then seasoned. Once Tumbleweed flowers, the leaves quickly age and become more fibrous and spiky, and generally less palatable.

Medicinal Uses
There is no medicinal use for Tumbleweed.

Cautions
There are no cautions for Tumbleweed.

Special Note
Tumbleweed really does tumble. Once this annual dies, the small taproot becomes brittle and eventually breaks, leaving the large clustered ball–like foliage to roll in the wind: across roads, lots, and Wild West movie scenes.

Tumbleweed is in the same family as Amaranth and Lambsquarters (Amaranthaceae). I consider it the least palatable of the bunch.

Sustenance Index: Low
Pictured: *Salsola tragus*

Watercress

Rorippa nasturtium–aquaticum

Other Common Names
Creek mustard, Berro

Range & Habitat
Common throughout most of North America, look for this naturalized semi–aquatic perennial along gently flowing streams and springs.

Edible Uses
Like other mustards, Watercress makes a nice addition to foraged salads and mixed greens. It is warming and spicy, and as an accent, is pleasantly stimulating to the palate. But most people find a mouth full of only Watercress too spicy. Larger quantities can be eaten if first boiled or steamed.

Medicinal Uses
A small handful is useful for stomach bloating and indigestion.

Cautions
Large amounts of Watercress can irritate the kidneys, and in some women, stimulate menses.

Special Note
Watercress (like London rocket) is one of the better tasting mustards. It has a well–deserved reputation as a leafy edible. Unlike true Mustard (Brassica or Sinapis), which is best known as the seed (and Mustard greens) source for the condiment, Watercress has a longer picking/eating season due to the extra hydration provided by its moist environs.

Before collecting any water–thriving plant, be aware of the water's quality. Agricultural/industrial runoff, cattle activity, and so on, can adversely affect the water, local plant life, and then the consumer. If microorganisms are suspected, a diluted chlorine bleach soak then rinse is wise.

Sustenance Index: Low
Pictured: *Rorippa nasturtium–aquaticum*

Wild Gourd

Cucurbita spp.

Other Common Names
Coyote gourd, Buffalo gourd, Desert gourd, Finger–leaf gourd

Range & Habitat
Common throughout mid and low elevations of the Sonoran Desert (and the Greater Southwest), Wild gourd is most often found growing along stream and wash margins, or on flats, in pastures, and along roadsides.

Edible Uses
Wild gourd should be picked when fully mature (yet still green or just beginning to yellow). Crack the gourd open by stepping on it and then remove the seeds. Spread the seeds out on a flat area (the adhering pulp will be removed later) and allow them to dry – a dehydrator or full sun will speed this process. Once dry, rub away any adhering dried gourd pulp. Finally, give the seeds a good water rinse to remove any residual bitterness from the inner gourd pulp.

With a little oil, lay the seeds out on a baking tray. Roast the seeds in an oven at about 350 degrees until they just begin to brown.

They are a good tasting pumpkin seed alternative. Filled with healthful oils (essential fatty acids), minerals, and protein, they make a fine addition to any wild food diet.

Medicinal Uses
The ample root, as with most Wild gourd types, can be used to make a weak soap solution. Containing large amounts of saponins the dried/fresh root is lathered in water and used for its detergent effect.

Cautions
There are no cautions for the seeds.

Sustenance Index: High
Pictured: *Cucurbita foetidissima* (top) | *C. foetidissima* raw gourd/roasted seeds (bottom)

Wild Lettuce
Lactuca serriola

Other Common Names
Prickly lettuce

Range & Habitat
A Eurasian native, Wild lettuce is found throughout North America. Lactuca serriola is the most commonly encountered species in the area. Look for the plant next to drainage areas, washsides, streamsides, cattle tanks, and other moistened and disturbed soils.

Edible Uses
As a relative of Lactuca sativa, or Garden lettuce, Wild lettuce has some related edibility – but with some minor drawbacks. The plant is bitter and prickly. The young, first emerging leaves are the easiest to work with: collect and boil the leaves at least once, though often two changes of water will be needed to remove the leaves' bitterness (and to soften the prickles). As a cooked green, it will be better in combination with other greens, or in limited quantities, as a soup addition.

Medicinal Uses
Wild lettuce is a mild sedative; this effect is largely dependent on bitter principles that are eliminated through boiling.

Cautions
There are no cautions for small to moderate amounts. Large quantities (if still bitter) may produce relaxation.

Special Note
'Lactucarium' or 'Poor man's opium' is the dried white exudate from any number of Lettuce species. This material was once smoked (or taken internally via a tincture) as a weak muscular/cerebral sedative.

Sustenance Index: Low
Pictured: *Lactuca serriola*

Wild Oats

Avena fatua

Range & Habitat

An Old World grain that is extensively naturalized throughout the United States and Southwest, look for Wild oats in damp ditches, along roadsides, washsides, and around intermittent streams. Some ground moisture is important for its growth.

Edible Uses

Wild oats is ready to harvest (late spring) when its seed chaff begins to tan and becomes slightly inflated (it can be gathered when still green – just allow it to dry fully before processing).

Strip the seeds from the upper plant by grabbing low with thumb and forefinger and then pull up.

Removing/separating the chaff from the seed will take the greatest amount of work. Lacking a combine, all by–hand thrashing techniques are labor intensive.

One way is to tie a pile of unthrashed Wild oats in a sheet and beat the grain with sticks and such; then winnow in a light breeze. Repeat. Cook Wild oats like any other grain or utilize it after grinding as a flour or meal.

Medicinal Uses

Part mild stimulant, part sedative, and part restorative, immature Wild oats has a unique influence on the nervous system. Oatgrass, the leafy portion of Wild oats, is a mineral rich beverage tea.

Cautions

There are no cautions for Wild oats.

Special Note

Although smaller, Wild oats is nearly identical in taste to Common oats (*Avena sativa*). One easy identifier for Wild oats is the appearance of the mature seed and husk: dangling cockroaches.

Sustenance Index: High
Pictured: *Avena fatua*

Wild Rhubarb
Rumex hymenosepalus

Other Common Names
Desert rhubarb, Tanner's dock, Cañaigre

Range & Habitat
From Wyoming, southwest to California, throughout Arizona and New Mexico to Oklahoma and Texas, look for Wild rhubarb in sandy–loamy soils. In the Sonoran region the plant is common and always found next to washes and on flood plains.

Edible Uses
The young and succulent flowering stalks are cut, peeled, and eaten as they stand. They are tart–tasting, hydrated, and refreshing.

The peeled stalks can also be stewed and used like true Rhubarb. I have sampled pies made with Wild rhubarb as a base filling and their quality tends to depend on the maker's expertise. I will say the defining ingredient in their creation is...sugar, and lots of it. The young–emerging leaves are eaten after a boil and water rinse.

Medicinal Uses
Due to their high tannin content, the tubers can be poulticed and applied to cuts and scrapes. The mature leaves will also make a soothing poultice for sunburn.

Cautions
Eating excess Wild rhubarb can cause intestinal upset; this is not a problem with eating occasional amounts.

Special Note
The tubers are often cited as a food source. Due to their great tannin content, rendering them palatable would take numerous boiling/straining/leaching rounds. A survival food, maybe, but the tubers certainly are not at the top of the list of preferred food plants.

Sustenance Index: Medium
Pictured: *Rumex hymenosepalus*

Wild Sunflower

Helianthus annuus

Other Common Names

Western sunflower, Arizona sunflower, etc.

Range & Habitat

Wild Sunflower is common throughout most of the Southwest (and from coast to coast). Locales just above desert elevations (and higher) are good places to look for the plant: roadsides, trailsides, forest openings, and meadows.

Edible Uses

Clip the seed heads from the upper stems when they are almost fully mature and dry. After drying in a paper bag or box, garble the seeds from the seed head. Eat as is (thin hull and all) or grind/sift and utilize the seeds as a meal. High in protein and essential oils, they are very nutritious.

Medicinal Uses

There are no medicinal uses for Wild sunflower.

Cautions

There are no cautions for Wild sunflower.

Special Note

Wild species are also a favorite of birds – if you wait until the seed heads are completely dry on the plant before collecting, they will be eaten.

Garden varieties of Sunflower are cultivars. They have been selected and bred over the years to produce the sunflower seed of commerce.

Jerusalem artichoke is also a Sunflower (Helianthus tuberosus) of sorts. But unlike Wild sunflower, Jerusalem artichoke is cultivated for its edible tuberous roots.

Sustenance Index: High
Pictured: *Helianthus annuus*

Wolfberry
Lycium spp.

Other Common Names
Desert thorn, Thornbush, Tomatillo

Range & Habitat
Wolfberry is found throughout low and mid elevations of the Southwest. It is a common Sonoran Desert perennial bush. Exposed flats, valleys, and hillsides are usual places for Wolfberry.

Edible Uses
The raw berries can be eaten in limited quantities (1 cup or so at a time), more so if first dried or stewed. A bland–sweetish to slightly bitter tasting fruit, Wolfberry is distinctly nightshade in taste. It's a good base material for jams and jellies. It also combines well with Ground cherry and Pápalo as a salsa ingredient.

Medicinal Uses
Wolfberry leaf is one of our better plant medicines for the watery eyes/runny nose of hayfever season.

Cautions & Special Note
Eat too much of the fruit and a short–term medicinal effect may be noticed – dry mouth, sinuses, eyes, and GI tract.

There are a variety of related plants growing throughout the Sonoran Desert. From shrubs (Wolfberry), small trees (Tree tobacco), and large perennial herbs (Datura) to smaller annuals/perennials (Ground cherry), make certain of proper identification before utilizing any nightshade. Wolfberry and Ground cherry are edible. Tree tobacco and Datura are non–edible and are generally considered poisonous (or strong plant medicines).

Goji berry (Lycium barbarum) is an Asian species of Wolfberry. It has been used for centuries in Traditional Chinese Medicine, and recently, as a popular dried snack fruit high in antioxidants. Native species of Wolfberry are likely similar in nutritional aspects.

Sustenance Index: Medium

Pictured: *Lycium exsertum* (top) | *Lycium andersonii* (bottom)

Yellowshow
Amoreuxia palmatifida

Other Common Names
Mexican yellowshow, Santa Rita yelllowshow, Saiya

Range & Habitat
Essentially a Mexico–centered species, Yellowshow's northern limit reaches into southern Arizona (and scarcely, southern New Mexico). The plant is mostly found in and around the Santa Rita, Atascosa, and Patagonia Mountains of Pima and Santa Cruz Counties. Responding to summer rains, during late July to August, look to upper desert and middle elevation southern exposures on rocky hillsides and foothills.

Edible Uses
Largely used south of the border, Yellowshow has a rich history as a wild food plant. Nearly all parts are edible. Gather the mild–tasting young leaves and green/immature inflated seedpods early in the season. These parts can be eaten fresh, or served as a cooked green. Once the small seeds mature, they darken in color, and are eaten as encountered as a crunchy snack. They can also be further prepared through roasting, parching, and/or grinding, and utilized accordingly. The roasted seed was once used as a coffee substitute.

The roots too are technically edible; however, in Arizona they tend to be small and tough, due to the plant being on the edge of its range. Also, even though Yellowshow is regionally abundant, it still is isolated and endemic in America. I believe it is best to utilize its above ground portions only and leave the roots untouched. This practice will help to keep native populations intact.

Medicinal Uses, Cautions, & Special Note
Yellowshow has no significant medicinal use and is caution free. Amoreuxia gonzalezii, a rare Yellowshow species, is infrequently found in the same areas as A. palmatifida. Its seedpods are more narrow and tapering. This species should be visually admired only.

Sustenance Index: High
Pictured: *Amoreuxia palmatifida*

Yucca (Fruit)
Yucca baccata, Y. schottii, Y. schidigera, etc.

Other Common Names
Banana yucca, Mountain yucca, Mohave yucca

Range & Habitat
Yucca baccata has the widest south-western range of the large fruit–bearing Yuccas. It includes southern California, southern Nevada, southern Utah, southern Colorado, and much of Arizona, New Mexico, and western Texas. It tends to flourish in upland areas of the Sonoran Desert.

Edible Uses
The fruit of all large fruit–bearing Yucca species are edible (as opposed to woody–fruit types like Joshua tree yucca and Soaptree yucca – see P. 61).

When ripe, brown spots of sugar fermentation will be notable on the skin's light green surface. Also look for animal gnaw marks.

Peel away the outer green skin. Slice the fruit open and discard the seeds. Eaten raw, the fruit's thin inner flesh is sweet. Fruit slices can also be wrapped in foil and roasted for 20–30 minutes over campfire coals. They will be syrupy and delicious. The young flowers too can be tried as a raw/cooked edible. Often a little bitter–soapy, they tend to be hit or miss in terms of palatability.

Medicinal Uses & Cautions
The roots are a common herbal remedy for arthritis. The seeds will cause gastrointestinal upset. If the fruit is found acrid and non–sweet, it has not fully ripened.

Special Note
The edible root of 'Yuca' (aka Cassava root or Manioc) is unrelated to Yucca – just a name similarity.

Sustenance Index: High
Pictured: *Yucca schottii* (top) | *Yucca schidigera* (bottom)

Yucca (Stalk)

Yucca glauca, Y. elata, Y. brevifolia, etc.

Other Common Names

Soapweed yucca, Soaptree yucca, Joshua tree, etc.

Range & Habitat

Yucca elata is just one common stalk–oriented species found in parts of the Sonoran Desert (though technically it is more closely associated with the Chihuahuan Desert).

Edible Uses

The immature stalks from any species of Yucca can be harvested for food – even the sweet–fruited species. As with most wild edible plants, Yucca's palatability has much to do with collection timing.

The immature and flexible stalk's last foot or so will be the best tasting. Further along towards the base it becomes more fibrous, bitter, and soapy. Cut the stalk from the plant's leafing top (if it is even slightly woody the 1–2 week window has been missed). Strip away the outer skin, exposing the inner core. Eat the inner stalk raw (limited), or better yet, boil, rinse, and season the material as a wild vegetable. This process also helps to remove any saponin–related bitterness that is common to Yucca.

Medicinal Uses

Yucca root preparations are a standard herbal treatment for arthritis.

Cautions & Special Note

Be aware of possible stomach upset with the ingestion of excess raw material. Considered inferior to Agave, Yucca's leaf fibers (most species) can be utilized in a similar fashion for cordage. The fruit of woody–capsule types (Joshua tree yucca, Chaparral yucca, etc.) are inedible. A weak soap solution is made from the roots.

Sustenance Index: Medium
Pictured: *Yucca elata*

Index